Written by Tammi Salzano and Heather Dakota
Designed by Michelle Martinez Design, Inc.
Cover by Bill Henderson

an imprint of
■SCHOLASTIC
www.scholastic.com

Scholastic and Tangerine Press and associated logos are trademarks of Scholastic Inc.
Published by Tangerine Press, an imprint of Scholastic Inc., 557 Broadway; New York, NY 10012

10 9 8 7 6 5 4 3 2 1
ISBN: 978-0-545-20289-3
Printed and bound in China

NOTE TO PARENTS:
Under each animal name, you will find
a scientific name. Though your young
reader may not be able to read Latin,
he or she will enjoy hearing you try!

PHOTO CREDITS:

P1, © Gary Bell/OceanwideImages.com;
P2, Trapdoor spider, © Andrew Williams/
critterzone.com; Mangrove snake, © Dorling
Kindersley/Getty Images; P5 © Dennis
Sheridan/critterzone.com; P7, © Robert
Barber/critterzone.com; P8&9, © Andrew
Williams/critterzone.com; P11, © Robert
Barber/critterzone.com; P13, © Gary Bell/
oceanwideimages.com; P15, © James VanZetta/
critterzone.com; P17, © Dennis Sheridan/
critterzone.com; P19, © Dorling Kindersley/
Getty Images; P21, © Dennis Sheridan/
critterzone.com; P23 Istock photo; P25, ©
Andrew Williams/critterzone.com; P26&27,
© Gary Bell/OceanwideImages.com; P29,
© Andrew Williams/critterzone.com; P31, ©
Andrew Williams/critterzone.com; P32&33,
© Andrew Williams/critterzone.com; P35, ©
Andrew Williams/critterzone.com; P37, Istock
photo; P39, © Troy Bartlett/critterzone.com;
P41, © Andrew Williams/critterzone.com; P43,
Istock photo; P45, © Troy Bartlett/critterzone.
com; P47, © Troy Bartlett/critterzone.com; P49,
© David Fleetham/SeaPic.com;
P51, © Anup Shah/Getty Images; P53, © Joe
McDonald/Corbis; P54, © Ralf Kiefner/SeaPic.
com; P55, © Dorothy Cutter/critterzone.com;
P57, © John Gordon/critterzone.com; P59,
© Clay Bryce/SeaPics.com; P61 © Dorothy
Cutter/critterzone.com; P63, © James Forte/
critterzone.com; P65, © Dorothy Cutter/
critterzone.com; P67, © Brian Jorg/critterzone.
com; P69, © Avi Klapfer/SeaPic.com; P71, ©
Doug Perrine/SeaPic.com, P73, © Ralf Kiefner/
SeaPic.com; P75, © JerryBargar/critterzone.
com; P77, © David Nasser/critterzone.com; P79,
© John Gordon/critterzone.com; P81, © James
Forte/critterzone.com; P83, © John Gordon/
critterzone.com; P85, © Dorothy Cutter/
critterzone.com; P87, © Eric Engbretson/
critterzone.com; P88, Istock photo; P89, ©
Andrew Williams/critterzone.com; P91, ©
Andrew Williams/critterzone.com; P92&93,
© Andrew Williams/critterzone.com; P95,
© Andrew Williams/critterzone.com; P96, ©
Andrew Williams/critterzone.com

Scholastic Canada Ltd.
Markham, Ontario

Scholastic Australia Pty. Ltd
Gosford, NSW

Scholastic New Zealand Ltd.
Greenmount, Auckland

WHAT IS POISON?

Poison is a substance that hurts or kills a living thing.

Many animals and bugs are born with *poison* in their bodies. This poison is called *venom*. The animals use the venom to kill prey or defend themselves. A creature that does this is *venomous* (VEN-um-iss).

Venomous animals use special body parts to deliver poison. They may have fangs, a stinger, *tentacles*, or a strawlike beak called a *proboscis* (pro-BOS-iss). Some venom hurts the heart or lungs. Other venom harms the blood.

LAND ANIMALS

In this book, you will learn about some **venomous creatures**.

You will find out where they live, what they eat, and how big they grow. Get ready to explore the world of poison!

FAST FACT

Venomous animals have poison in their bodies and *inject* it into their prey. **Poisonous** animals have poison in their bodies, but they can't deliver it. An animal that eats a poisonous creature, like a toad, will become sick or even die.

Trapdoor Spider

Numbers: hundreds of different kinds

Where found: all over the world

Mangrove Snake

All of these animals live on land. Most live on the ground all the time. Others are found in trees and in the water, too! About ⅓ of all the animals in the world live on land.

GILA MONSTER

(Heloderma suspectum)

◎ Gila monsters are the only venomous lizards found in the United States.

◎ The Gila monster puts venom into its victim by biting it with sharp teeth. As the Gila monster chews, it injects even more venom!

◎ Gila monsters can go for months without food. They live off of fat stored in their tail.

FAST FACTS

Length: 18 to 22 inches (46 to 55 cm)

Weight: about 3 pounds (1.3 kg)

Color: black, pink, and yellow beadlike, scaly skin

Food: small *mammals*, birds, lizards, frogs, and eggs

Where found: deserts in Mexico and the United States

MONITOR LIZARDS

(Varanus)

◎ Monitor lizards are related to the mosasaur (MOH-suh-sawr). The mosasaur lived during the time of the dinosaurs.

◎ A monitor lizard has a long, forked tongue and a powerful tail.

◎ Monitor lizards inject venom by biting their victims with sharp teeth.

The largest monitor lizard is the Komodo dragon. It can weigh up to 365 pounds (165 kg)!

FAST FACTS

Length: 8 inches to 13 feet (20 cm to 4 m)

Color: many different colors

Food: small mammals, reptiles, reptile eggs, birds, insects, and *carrion* (dead animals)

Where found: Africa, Asia, East Indies, and Australia

RATTLESNAKE

(Crotalus, Sistrurus)

◎ Rattlesnakes have long fangs. They use the fangs to inject venom into their prey.

◎ An adult rattlesnake eats about every two weeks.

◎ Rattlesnakes are pit vipers. They have holes (pits) on their head that sense the body heat of their prey.

FAST FACTS

Length: 1 foot to 8 feet (0.3 to 2.4 m)

Color: many different shades and patterns of brown

Food: rabbits, squirrels, mice, rats, frogs, and lizards

Where found: North, Central, and South America

BLACK MAMBA

(Dendroaspis polylepsis)

◎ Black mambas are the fastest moving snakes in the world. They can travel 12½ miles per hour (20 kph).

◎ The black mamba injects venom into its prey using sharp fangs.

◎ When a black mamba gets scared, it can raise its body and head 4 feet (1.2 m) off the ground.

The black mamba gets its name from the black color on the inside of its mouth.

FAST FACTS

Length: 14 feet (4.5 m)

Color: gray or olive green

Food: mice, squirrels, birds, frogs, and lizards

Where found: Africa

INLAND TAIPAN

(Oxyuranus microlepidotus)

◎ The inland taipan is the most venomous land snake in the world.

◎ Inland taipans inject venom with long, sharp fangs.

◎ Like all snakes, the inland taipan keeps growing its entire life.

FAST FACTS

Length: 6½ feet (2 m)

Color: dark tan or brownish olive-green

Food: small rodents (mainly rats)

Where found: Australia

COPPERHEAD

(Agkistrodon contortrix)

◎ When copperheads sense danger, they stop moving. They stay motionless until the threat passes.

◎ A copperhead puts venom into its victim by biting it with long fangs.

◎ A female copperhead can lay as many as 20 eggs at a time.

FAST FACTS

Length: 2 to 3 feet (0.6 to 0.9 m)

Color: copper with darker bands

Food: mice, voles, frogs, lizards, birds, and bugs

Where found: United States and Mexico

KING COBRA

(Ophiophagus hannah)

◎ King cobras have fangs that don't fold up into the snake's mouth. They bite their prey with the fangs to inject venom.

◎ The king cobra is the longest venomous snake. Some are as long as a car!

◎ These snakes are excellent swimmers.

FAST FACTS

Length: 13 to 18 feet (4 to 5.5 m)

Color: yellow, green, brown, or black; light yellow throat

Food: other snakes, lizards, rodents, and birds

Where found: India, southern China, and Southeast Asia

MANGROVE SNAKE

(Boiga dendrophila)

◎ The mangrove snake has small fangs in the back of its mouth. The snake bites its victim to inject venom.

◎ Mangrove snakes are good swimmers.

◎ Mangrove snakes are also known as yellow-ringed cat snakes.

FAST FACTS

Length: 6 to 8 feet (1.8 to 2.4 m)

Color: black with yellow bands

Food: birds and bird eggs, frogs, rodents, bats, and other snakes

Where found: Southeast Asia and India

CORAL SNAKE

(Leptomicrurus micrurus)

◉ Coral snakes belong to the same family as cobras.

◉ A coral snake bites its prey with small fangs to inject venom.

◉ Coral snakes are *nocturnal*. This mean they are active at night.

FAST FACTS

Length: 2 feet (0.6 m)

Color: black, yellow, and red bands

Food: other snakes, rats, mice, and lizards

Where found: all over the world

GREEN BAMBOO VIPER
(Trimeresurus stejnegeri)

- This snake delivers poison with long fangs.

- It moves slowly, but is very aggressive.

- Green bamboo vipers have red eyes.

FAST FACTS

Length: 20 to 30 inches (50 to 76 cm)

Color: green with a red tail

Food: rodents, lizards, and birds

Where found: Southeast China, Thailand, Vietnam, India, and Taiwan

BLACK WIDOW SPIDER

(Latrodectus)

◎ Black widow spiders put venom into their prey by biting it with their fangs.

◎ Drop for drop, a black widow's venom is stronger than a rattlesnake's venom.

◎ Only female black widows are dangerous to humans. Males and young black widows are harmless.

FAST FACTS

Length: ¾ inch to 1½ inches (2 to 3.8 cm)

Color: shiny black body; females have a red hourglass shape on their belly

Food: insects

Where found: warm parts of the world

Spiders don't have teeth for chewing food. They use their fangs to inject venom into their prey. This turns their victim's insides into liquid. The spider then slurps up its meal.

SYDNEY FUNNEL-WEB SPIDER

(Atrax robustus)

◎ The Sydney funnel-web is the most dangerous spider in the world to humans. A single bite can kill if the wound is not treated.

◎ This spider uses its long fangs to inject venom into prey.

◎ The Sydney funnel-web lives in a hole under rocks or logs. It puts silk lines outside the hole to catch prey. The victim trips on the silk line. Then, the spider rushes out of the hole to grab its meal.

FAST FACTS

Length: ½ inch to 1½ inches (1.3 to 3.8 cm)

Color: shiny dark brown or black

Food: small lizards, snails, beetles, and cockroaches

Where found: Australia

GOLIATH BIRD EATER

(Theraphosa blondi)

- ◎ Goliath bird eaters are tarantulas (hairy spiders). They are the largest tarantulas in the world.

- ◎ These spiders rarely eat birds, but they are big enough to do so!

- ◎ The Goliath bird eater kills its victim by injecting venom with its fangs.

FAST FACTS

Length: 12-inch (30-cm) leg span

Weight: 2½ ounces (70 g)

Color: light and dark brown

Food: frogs, small snakes, lizards, beetles, insects, bats, and birds

Where found: South America

TRAPDOOR SPIDER
(Ctenizidae)

◎ A trapdoor spider lives in a *burrow* (a hole in the ground). It covers the burrow with dirt, grass, and silk to make a trap door. When prey comes by, the spider grabs it.

◎ These spiders inject venom into their prey by biting it with their fangs.

◎ There are 120 different kinds of trapdoor spiders.

FAST FACTS

Length: ¼ to ¾ inch (6.5 to 19 mm)

Color: black or brown with spotty markings

Food: small birds, small snakes, mice, small fish, frogs, and insects

Where found: Africa, Japan, South America, and North America

BROWN RECLUSE SPIDER

(Loxosceles reclusa)

◎ Most spiders have four pairs of eyes. The brown recluse has three pairs.

◎ Brown recluse spiders inject venom into their prey with tiny fangs.

◎ The brown recluse spider lives in small, dark places.

FAST FACTS

Length: ¼ to ¾ inch (6.5 to 19 mm)

Color: golden brown with a dark-brown or black fiddle shape on the head

Food: insects

Where found: United States

WOLF SPIDER

(Lycosidae)

- ◎ There are more than 2,000 different kinds of wolf spiders in the world.

- ◎ The wolf spider hunts its prey by running after it.

- ◎ Wolf spiders have fangs. They bite their victims to inject venom.

FAST FACTS

Length: ⅕ inch to 3 inches (1 to 8 cm)

Color: dark brown

Food: insects and other spiders

Where found: all over the world

DADDY LONG-LEGS SPIDER

(Pholcus phalangioides)

◎ Daddy longlegs spiders inject venom with short fangs.

◎ After the female lays her eggs, she wraps them in silk and carries them in her jaws until they hatch.

◎ This spider is almost see-through. If you use a microscope, you can see the blood cells moving in its body!

FAST FACTS

Length: ¼ to ⅓ inch (6 to 8 mm)

Color: pale yellow-brown with a gray patch on the head and *thorax*

Food: insects and other spiders

Where found: all over the world

Two other creatures, craneflies and harvestmen, also are called *daddy longlegs*. These animals are not spiders.

BULLET ANT

(Paraponera clevata)

◎ Bullet ants deliver poison with a stinger. The sting is extremely painful.

◎ If these ants bite something too hard to be crushed by their jaws, the force hurls them into the air!

◎ When a bullet ant bites, its jaws spring shut at more then 60 miles per hour (97 kph).

FAST FACTS

Length: 1 inch (2.5 cm)

Color: reddish-black

Food: insects (mainly termites) and flower *nectar*

Where found: rain forests in Central and South America

CENTIPEDE

(Chilopoda)

◎ Centipedes are nocturnal.

◎ A centipede injects venom into its victim with its fangs.

◎ Centipedes are the only insects that have fangs.

The word *centipede* means "one hundred feet." Many centipedes have fewer than that. Some have more!

FAST FACTS

Length: 1 inch to 3 feet (2.5 cm to 1 m)

Color: pale yellow to dark brown

Food: spiders, slugs, earthworms, and insects

Where found: warm parts of the world

DEATH STALKER SCORPION

(Leiurus quinquestriatus)

◎ Death stalkers are the most venomous scorpions on Earth.

◎ The death stalker delivers venom with a stinger at the tip of its tail.

◎ Death stalkers hunt at night.

FAST FACTS

Length: 3½ to 4½ inches (9 to 11.5 cm)

Color: tan or reddish-brown with a black stinger and pincer tips

Food: spiders, crickets, flies, and moths

Where found: deserts in northern Africa and the Middle East

PUSS MOTH CATERPILLAR

(Megalopyge opercularis)

◎ The puss moth caterpillar injects venom through hollow hairs. The hairs are attached to poison sacs on its body.

◎ The puss moth is one of the most *toxic* caterpillars in North America.

◎ Puss moth caterpillars can sting even after they're dead! The venom in the hollow hairs still can be injected into a person's skin if the caterpillar is picked up.

FAST FACTS

Length: 1 inch to 1½ inches (2.5 to 3.8 cm)

Color: brown, tan, or gray

Food: plants, trees, leaves, and shrubs

Where found: southern United States and Mexico

A caterpillar is the *larva* (early form) of a moth or butterfly.

SADDLEBACK CATERPILLAR

(Sibine stimulea)

◎ The saddleback caterpillar has horns on its front and back ends.

◎ A saddleback injects venom through hollow hairs. The hairs are attached to poison sacs on the caterpillar's body.

◎ The front and back ends of saddleback caterpillars look the same. This makes it hard for *predators* to know where to attack.

FAST FACTS

Length: 1 inch (2.5 cm)

Color: purplish-brown body with a green saddle shape on the back; dark purple spot in the middle of the "saddle"

Food: tree and shrub leaves

Where found: eastern North America

PLATYPUS

(Ornithorhynchus anatinus)

◎ Scientists studying the platypus have discovered that the platypus is a strange combination of mammal, reptile, and bird.

◎ This unique animal has a bill like a duck, a tail like a beaver, and feet like an otter.

◎ The male platypus has a spike on his hind foot. The spike is used to inject venom, usually in self-defense or when fighting other males.

FAST FACTS

Length: 16 to 24 inches (41 to 61 cm)

Weight: 2 to 5 pounds (0.9 to 2 kg)

Color: waterproof dark brown fur; gray-blue bill

Food: shrimp, snails, crayfish, insects, and worms

Where found: Australia

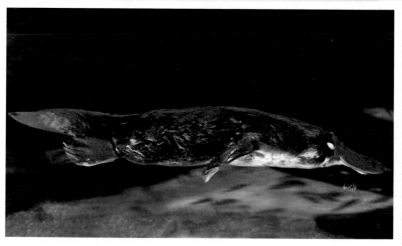

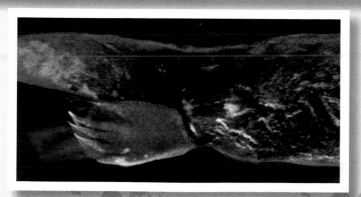

SLOW LORIS

(Nycticebus coucang)

◎ Slow lorises have venom in the glands of their inner elbows. They mix this venom with their saliva. Then, they deliver the venom by biting.

◎ The venom has a strong, unpleasant odor. Mothers cover their babies with the venom to keep predators away.

◎ Slow lorises are *arboreal* (are-bore-E-al). This means they live in trees.

FAST FACTS

Length: 8 to 15 inches (21 to 38 cm)

Weight: about 4½ pounds (2 kg)

Color: brown or reddish-brown fur

Food: small mammals, baby birds, bird eggs, insects, and fruit

Where found: Southeast Asia

SHORT-TAILED SHREW
(Blarina)

◎ Short-tailed shrews need to eat their weight in food every day.

◎ These animals are good diggers and swimmers.

◎ Short-tailed shrews have venom in the glands of their lower jaw. This venom mixes with their saliva. They deliver the venom by biting.

FAST FACTS

Length: 3½ inches (8.8 cm)

Weight: less than 1 ounce (14 g)

Color: gray-brown fur

Food: mice, lizards, worms, snails, insects, nuts, and berries

Where found: United States and Canada

SEA ANIMALS

There are animals in the sea that have venom, too.

Venomous creatures include jellyfish, octopuses, and certain fish. Some, like sea snakes, live where it's warm. Others, like the Arctic jellyfish, live where it's cold.

Numbers:
about 1,000 different kinds of venomous fish

9,000 different kinds of venomous *invertebrates* (animals without a backbone)

Where found:
in waters all over the world

Portuguese Man-of-War

- The most venomous animal on Earth lives in the sea. It's the box jellyfish.

- Many sea creatures use venom to defend themselves or to hunt prey.

- Sea creatures release their poison by touching (like a Portuguese man-of-war) or injecting (like a snake).

- Venomous sea creatures usually don't attack unless they get scared.

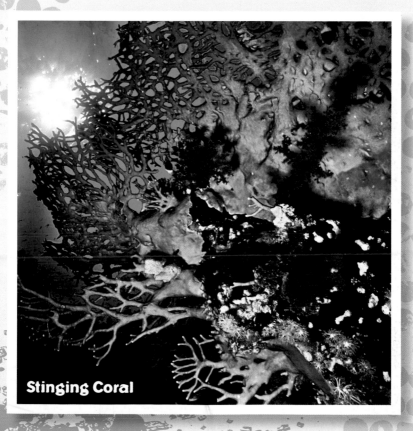

Stinging Coral

BOX JELLYFISH

(also called a *sea wasp* and a *marine stinger*)
(*Chironex fleckeri*)

- The venom of the box jellyfish is the deadliest in the animal kingdom.

- Sea turtles are not hurt by the box jellyfish's sting. The turtles eat the jellyfish!

- The box jellyfish has 60 tentacles that can grow to be 15 feet (4.5 m) long.

- The body is large and shaped like a box.

Box jellyfish have up to 5,000 stinging cells on their tentacles. The cells shoot out like darts.

FAST FACTS

Length: the bell (body) can get as big as a basketball

Color: clear pale blue

Food: small fish and shellfish

Where found: Australia, the Philippines, and tropical seas

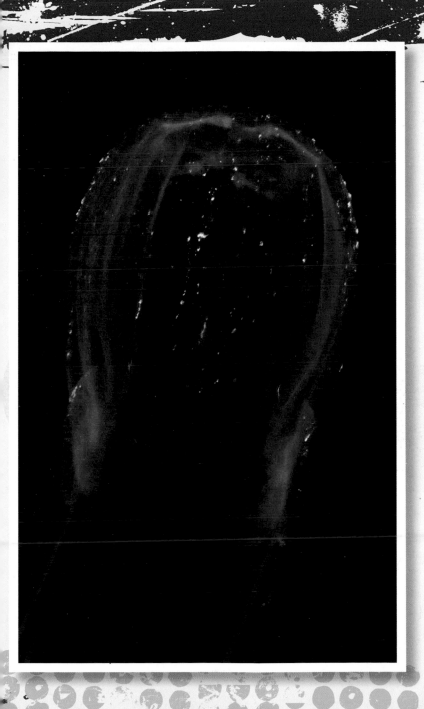

BLUE-RINGED OCTOPUS

(Hapalochlaena)

◎ There are about 10 different kinds of blue-ringed octopus.

◎ The venom is made by bacteria in the octopus's saliva.

◎ Octopuses live for only about two years.

◎ The blue-ringed octopus has green blood, three hearts, and eight arms.

FAST FACTS

Length: 4½ to 6 inches (12 to 15 cm)

Color: *camouflaged* until scared, then it turns yellow with blue rings or lines

Food: small crabs and shrimp

Where found: tidal pools in Japan and Australia

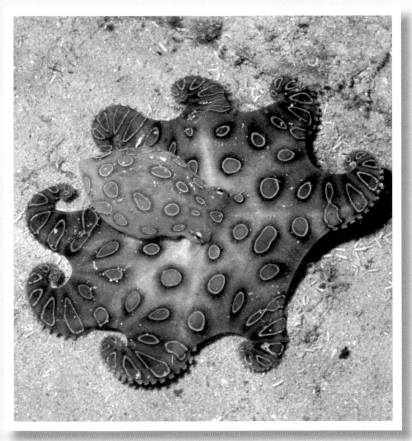

STONEFISH

(Synanceia verrucosa)

- ◎ The stonefish lives on the bottom of the reef bed.

- ◎ Stonefish have venomous spines on their back.

- ◎ It's the most venomous fish.

FAST FACTS

Length: 13½ to 19½ inches (35 to 50 cm)

Color: camouflaged, many different colors

Food: small fish and shrimp

Where found: coral reefs in the Pacific and Indian Oceans

SEA SNAKES

(Elapidae)

◎ Sea snakes breathe air.

◎ The flat tail of the sea snake helps it to swim.

◎ Sea snakes can stay underwater for a few hours.

◎ These snakes have short fangs and very toxic venom.

The most venomous sea snake is the beaded sea snake.

FAST FACTS

Length: 4 to 5 feet (1.2 to 1.5 m)

Color: many different colors and patterns

Food: fish, fish eggs, and eels

Where found: warm, shallow waters in the Indian and Pacific Oceans

STINGRAY
(Dasyatidae)

- ◎ Stingrays are a type of fish. They are related to sharks.

- ◎ Rays move their wings to glide through the water.

- ◎ The stinger is a razor-sharp spine that grows at the end of the tail.

- ◎ Stingrays bury themselves in the sand to hide and hunt for prey.

FAST FACTS

Length: 5 inches to 6½ feet (12.5 cm to 2 m)

Color: gray and brown; some have patterns

Food: fish, fish eggs, and eels

Where found: Atlantic, Pacific, and Indian Oceans

Ancient Greek dentists used stingray venom to numb patients so they would not feel pain.

PUFFERFISH

(Tetraodontidae)

◎ Its skin and some internal organs are poisonous to humans.

◎ Pufferfish swim very slowly.

◎ The pufferfish can move each eye separately.

◎ A pufferfish can look like a big balloon by filling its stomach with water.

FAST FACTS

Length: up to 20 inches (51 cm)

Color: bright colors in many different patterns

Food: algae, seaweed, clams, shrimp, scallops, and mussels

Where found: near the shore, from the Atlantic Ocean to the Pacific Ocean

Ancient Egyptians used pufferfish as balls for a game of bowling!

SEA URCHIN

(Toxopneustes pileolus)

◎ Sea urchins hide in the holes in rocks during the day.

◎ Sea urchins look like balls or biscuits.

◎ They move by using their spines or tube feet.

◎ The sting of the flower urchin is very poisonous.

FAST FACTS

Length: 1 inch to 4 inches (3 to 10 cm)

Color: usually black, but can be purple, brown, or white

Food: kelp and *plankton*

Where found: in every ocean around the world

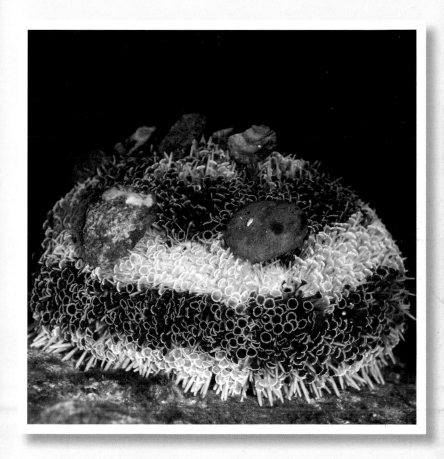

CONE SNAIL

(Conidae)

- ◎ There are more than 500 different kinds of cone snails.

- ◎ Cone snails move very slowly.

- ◎ A cone snail uses its venomous tongue with a harpoonlike tip to catch prey.

- ◎ Cone snails suck up water to smell prey.

FAST FACTS

Length: up to 6 inches (15 cm)

Color: usually brown and white patterned shells

Food: *marine* worms, small fish, mollusks, and other cone snails

Where found: reefs in the Indian and Pacific Oceans

PORTUGUESE MAN-OF-WAR

(Physalia physalis)

- ◎ Man-of-wars have an air bladder. This allows them to float on the ocean's surface.

- ◎ The venom is located on the tentacles.

- ◎ Portuguese man-of-wars are not jellyfish.

Its tentacles can reach 33 feet (10 m) in length!

FAST FACTS

Length: up to 170 feet (52 m)

Color: purplish-blue

Food: small fish and shrimp

Where found: warm waters throughout the world, and in the North Atlantic Gulf Stream

SCORPIONFISH

(Scorpaenidae)

◎ Scorpionfish have venomous spines all over their bodies.

◎ Some scorpionfish can change color to blend in with their surroundings. This is called camouflage.

◎ There are more than 1,000 different kinds of scorpionfish.

FAST FACTS

Length: up to 20 inches (51 cm)

Color: many different bright colors

Food: small fish

Where found: rocks and reefs of warm oceans; mostly found in the Pacific and Indian Oceans

TOADFISH

(Opsanus tau)

◎ Male toadfish "sing" to attract a female.

◎ A toadfish has hollow spines along its back and tail fin. The fish injects venom through the spines.

◎ Toadfish can live out of water for short periods of time.

FACTS

Length: about 1 foot (0.3 m)

Color: usually olive green, brown, or dull yellow

Food: fish, shrimp, and other small marine animals

Where found: near the bottom of waters along the coast of North America

LIONFISH

(Scorpaenidae)

- ◎ The lionfish is a type of scorpionfish.

- ◎ Lionfish will eat anything that they can get in their mouths.

- ◎ These fish are found around reefs and rocky crevices.

- ◎ Lionfish hunt at night.

FAST FACTS

Length: 12 to 15 inches (30 to 38 cm)

Color: red and white stripes

Food: fish and shrimp

Where found: warm oceans around the world

SEA CUCUMBER

(Holothuroidea)

- ◉ The sea cucumber has a soft, long body that looks like a cucumber.

- ◉ Sea cucumbers are found on the ocean floor.

- ◉ Sea cucumbers are related to starfish.

- ◉ These animals move by using small tubes on the bottom of their bodies.

FAST FACTS

Length: ½ inch to 3½ feet (1.3 cm to 1 m)

Color: many different colors

Food: plankton

Where found: tropical reefs around the world

When attacked, they let go of toxic, sticky threads, which are part of their guts. These regrow very quickly.

SEA ANEMONE

(also called *the flower of the sea*)

(Actiniaria)

◎ Sea anemones are related to jellyfish and corals.

◎ The sea anemone can have 10 to more than 100 tentacles.

◎ Sea anemones look like plants, but they are meat-eating animals.

◎ The sticky foot of the sea anemone attaches to rocks or coral.

FAST FACTS

Length: ½ inch to 6 feet (1.25 cm to 2 m) in diameter

Color: many different colors

Food: small fish and shrimp

Where found: oceans all over the world, but mostly in warmer climates

STINGING CORAL

(also called *fire coral*)

(Millepora)

◎ Stinging coral look like coral, but are related to jellyfish and sea anemone.

◎ This coral has a delicate fan shape.

◎ Stinging coral deliver venom with very small tentacles.

Fire coral *colonies* can grow to be 5 feet (1.5 m).

FAST FACTS

Length: each ⅛ inch to 2½ inches (3 to 56 mm) in diameter

Color: yellow, brown, red, white, orange, and green.

Food: plankton

Where found: Indian and Pacific Oceans

CATFISH

(Siluriformes)

- ◎ Catfish have a flat head. This allows them to dig for prey.

- ◎ These fish do not have scales.

- ◎ Most catfish have a bony, spinelike ray on their back and tail fin. The ray can deliver a nasty sting.

- ◎ The electric catfish of Africa can generate up to 350 volts of electricity.

FAST FACTS

Length: ½ inch to 10 feet (10 mm to 3 m)

Color: gray, blue, dark green, brown, white, peach, or yellow

Food: crayfish, clams, worms, insect larvae, and small fish

Where found: saltwater and freshwater on every continent, except Antarctica

A Mekong catfish was caught that weighed 646 pounds (293 kg)!

AIR ANIMALS

Some insects have venom in their bodies, too.
Insects have things in common with each other.

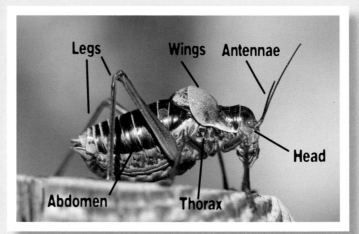

Legs   Wings   Antennae

Head

Abdomen   Thorax

- Insects have three body parts: head, thorax, and *abdomen*.

- Most have six legs.

- They have two antennae.

- Many have an *exoskeleton* (a hard covering on the outside of their body).

- Most have wings and can fly.

Numbers:
more than one
million different kinds

Where found:
all over the
world

Insects are very important. Some, like bees, help flowers make seeds for fruit or new plants. Others, like assassin bugs, eat other insects that can be pests.

Assassin Bug

WASP

(Vespidae)

- ◎ Many wasps build nests made of mud. Some wasps chew plants to make a cone-shaped, paperlike nest.

- ◎ Female wasps have a stinger attached to a venom sac on their bodies. They deliver the venom by stinging.

- ◎ There are about 5,000 different species of wasps in the world. Hornets and yellow jackets are two kinds.

FACTS

Length: less than ½ inch to 2 inches (1.3 to 5 cm)

Color: all different colors

Food: fruit, flower nectar, insects, and carrion

Where found: all over the world

HONEYBEE

(Apis mellifera)

◎ Female honeybees have a stinger attached to a venom sac on their bodies. They deliver the venom by stinging.

◎ A honeybee leaves its stinger and part of its body when it stings.

◎ Bees "dance" to show other bees where to find nectar.

FAST FACTS

Length: ⅖ to ⅝ inch (10 to 16 mm)

Color: golden brown and black

Food: flower nectar

Where found: all over the world

There are three types of bees: the queen, workers, and drones. The queen lays eggs. Workers are females that gather food, make honey, and protect the hive. Drones are males that mate with the queen.

ASSASSIN BUG

(Reduviidae)

- ◎ Assassin bugs are poor fliers.

- ◎ Assassin bugs have a proboscis , which is a strawlike beak. They stab their prey with the proboscis and inject venom. Then they slurp up their meal.

- ◎ If other food is not available, assassin bugs will eat each other.

FAST FACTS

Length: up to 1½ inches (3.8 cm)

Color: gray, green, orange, brown, black, or a combination of these

Food: other insects

Where found: all over the world

BUMBLEBEE

(Bombus)

- ◎ Female bumblebees have a stinger attached to a venom sac on their bodies. They deliver the venom by stinging.

- ◎ Unlike honeybees, bumblebees can sting more than once.

- ◎ Sometimes, bumblebees build a wax "roof" over their hive for protection.

FAST FACTS

Length: about ¾ inch (1.9 cm)

Color: fuzzy black and yellow hairs

Food: flower nectar

Where found: all over the world

GLOSSARY

Abdomen: the last section of a bug's body

Arboreal: refers to an animal that lives in trees

Burrow: a hole in the ground where an animal lives

Camouflage: to blend in with the surroundings in order to hide

Carrion: a dead animal

Colony: a large group of animals that live together

Exoskeleton: a hard covering on the outside of an animal's body

Inject: to force venom into prey

Invertebrate: an animal without a backbone

Larva: the young form of many insects

Mammal: animals, including humans, that have hair or fur and feed their babies milk

Marine: relating to the sea

Nectar: a sweet liquid made by some plants that is used to make honey

Nocturnal: active at night

Plankton: tiny, plantlike material found in the sea

Poison: a substance that hurts or kills a living thing

Poisonous: full of poison

Predator: an animal that lives by killing and eating other animals

Prey: an animal that is hunted and killed by another animal for food

Proboscis: a strawlike beak that some insects use to suck up food

Stinger: a sharp organ usually connected to a poison gland

Tentacles: armlike organs that some animals use to catch prey or move around

Thorax: the middle section of a bug's body

Toxic: harmful

Venom: poisonous matter that some animals use to kill prey

Venomous: full of poison